The Things We Did

Memories in Rhyme

LaDonna Hope Crawford

The Things We Did

Copyright © 2025 LaDonna Hope Crawford

Published by Kingdom Publishing Press

Franklin, Tennessee, USA

All rights reserved. No part of this publication may be reproduced, digitally stored, or transmitted in any form without the permission of Kingdom Publishing Press.

ISBN: 979-8-9933640-0-1

Printed in the United States of America

The Things We Did

Memories in Rhyme

To my family,

Thank you for the memories of the things we did.

Foreword

C.S. Lewis once wrote, "I must keep alive in myself the desire for my true country, which I shall not find till after death." While my mom told me many stories of growing up in the hills of Kentucky, her country, she never once put her nostalgia for her past above her desire for our "true country", our forever home with our Father, made accessible though our Lord Jesus Christ.

Memory is one of the most beautiful gifts given to us by our Father. Memory allows us to go back in time, to remember what it was like to see the ordinary things of *this* world for the very first time with childlike wonderment. There is something magical and mysterious about the stories of a place I would never really know—a past that cannot be relived, only retold. As far back as I can remember, mom told me the stories of her life on Peter Trace, taking me back to another time, in a seemingly other world—a world I think many long for, a time forgotten and overlooked by progress, technology, and myriads of modern distractions. Her recollections became a part of my own past, my growing up, my desire for the way things were—and sometimes I even imagined what it would have been like to be a character in her stories, watching from the woods as her adventures unfolded.

I am so, so thankful my mom agreed to share her memories in rhyme, so that those who find this piece of her can be whisked back to her country, where it was simply *The Things We Did*.

Table of Contents

Front Porch Preacher	3
Birthday Surprise	5
Lavender Shoes	7
Rainbow Cave	9
Old Whitey	11
The Sawmill	13
Barns	15
Bible Man	17
The Switchin'	19
Mr. Rooster's Demise	21
The Swimmin' Hole	23-24
Hornets' Nest	25
Green Onions	27
The Country Store	29-30
The Hickory Nut Tree	31
The Hog Lot	33
Canning Time	35
Secondhand Dresses	37
Little White Schoolhouse	39-40
Mad Dogs	41
Haunted House	43
The Frightful Pot Belly Stove	45
Mammy's Christmas Tree	47
Christmas at Mom-maw's	49
Santa Clause and the Old Smokehouse	51

Front Porch Preacher

I was enamored with the radio preaching so grand.
Mimicking him, I was his biggest fan.

There I stood on the front porch, pretending to preach,
listening to the radio preacher preach and weep.

Flailing my arms in earnest desire,
those watching, mouths ajar, listening to my fire.

Holding in their laughs, I must have been a sight to behold,
since I was only eight years old.

LHC

Birthday Surprise

A birthday surprise to come today!
Anticipation abounds as I play.

What could it be, something pretty, sparkly, and new?
A big box? A little box? With ribbons of blue?

My excitement grows and grows awaiting my birthday surprise.
At last! It's here! Before my very eyes!

Time to open and see inside the box…
Oh no! It's Bobbie socks!

LHC

Lavender Shoes

The catalog arrived, to my surprise!
Turned the page, lavender shoes inside!

Today my shoes arrived
with round pleated bows and heels a half inch high.

To my delight, they felt just fine,
my lavender shoes so divine.

The scent of leather so clean and new.
Oh, how I love my lavender shoes.

LHC

8

Rainbow Cave

Donny, Butch, Shirely, Gail, and I on an adventure we did go
to find the cave shaped like a rainbow.

Over the bridge and through the field,
we did trek up the hill.

Up, up we go, through the woods and up the hills so steep,
eyes searching, hearts pounding to find the cave we seek.

Legs so spent from climbing high,
out of breath we stop and sigh.

There beyond the trees we behold,
Rainbow Cave, so very old.

We ate our lunch inside the cave,
as we talked of our escapade.

Proud of our success, but now home we must go,
with thoughts of the cave shaped like a rainbow.

LHC

Old Whitey

I love to go to Grandpa's house every day,
but Old Whitey is always there to scare me away.

Coming over the hill my eyes search the yard
for Old Whitey lies there! I hope he is too tired…

to come chase me to the nearest car!
But no, here he comes with his growling snarl!

I shout for help to the nearest one,
to rescue me from Old Whitey's teethe and slobbery tongue!

LHC

The Sawmill

Just over the hill the sawmill grinds,
buzzing and singing a familiar tune we find.

Mules running down the hill, logs in tow.
Look out! We must go!

Sawdust whirling up in the sky,
as logs turn into boards a mile high!

Verdon, Donny, Butch, and Grandpa,
sawing logs from dawn to nightfall.

When the day is done and the sawdust deep,
we climb and play on the sawdust heap

I miss the sound of the sawmill's hum,
so long ago when I was young.

LHC

Barns

One old to hold the mules who kicked at their stalls,
one new holds a corn crib that feeds them all.

Newly sawed wood, we loved the smell.
From the beam at the center, our swing hung so well.

Swinging high to the rafters we went,
taking our breath with our descent.

In the barn we would play,
horseshoes every day.

In the fall, barn smells would change,
for tobacco from the rafters now did hang.

One old, one new…
I miss the barns that I once knew.

LHC

Bible Man

Each Sunday morning up the
hollar he came,
to pick up children for church
where Jesus was proclaimed.

From the backseat I could see,
in the mirror clear to me,
the Bible man, shedding tears
with a smile that showed no fear.

How could this be? Tears of joy, I decide,
because of the Savior for us who died.
Rose again, He did do,
to save our souls like me and you.

LHC

The Switchin'

On the way home down the holler
riding in the backseat, windows rolled down,
my sister and I hung our heads out looking at the ground.

Mom threatened our very lives,
when home we would arrive.

For disobeying hanging out the windows that day,
my sister and I were going to pay.

When out by the well box we did hide,
Mom fetching switches to sting our legs and hurt our pride.

Lesson learned that day,
Mind your mom or you will pay.

LHC

Mr. Rooster's Demise

While out to play one day, Shirley Ann came from the barn
was chased and ambushed by the biggest and meanest rooster on
the farm.

Upon her head he flew,
wings flapping and pecking too.
Screams were hard all over the farm
as Shirley Ann was flinging her arms.

Needless to say a rescue was in play
to save Shirley Ann from Mr. Rooster that day.
Shirley Ann survived the flogging,
but Mr. Rooster a fatal blow to his noggin!

It was no surprise at all,
that chicken and dumplings was for dinner y'all.

LHC

The Swimming Hole

We hurry down the path to our beloved swimming hole,
donning our old clothes and sneakers with holes.

We love to climb on the roots of the big old tree and dive in with excited glee!
What fun! What fun! To see the crawdads flee!

"Oh my! What's that crawlin' in my shoe?"
It's Mr. Crawdad and his family too!

Oh our swimming hole beneath the hillside bank
where we climbed and swung on grapevines until into the water
we sank.

Swimming hole full of crawdads, minnows, and snakes,
all take flight in our splashing wakes.

We swam with joy, till tired and frayed,

so off to the yard to blankets we did lay.

"Quick! Get the salt!" For June apples await.
Can't eat too many, or we'll end with a belly ache.

Sunshine, blankets, warm apples so filling. "What's that you say?"
"Get up it's time to go?"
Back down to the swimming hole.

LHC

Hornets' Nest

My sister and I, curious as can be,
found a big puffy gray thing we wanted to see.

"Is there something inside this gray puffy thing?"
As we took our sticks and began to sling.

Pounding the thing with might,
we heard buzzing sounds inside that would soon take flight.

"Hurry! Run!" Unhappy they are,
buzzing and swirling to chase us far.

My sister and I learned a lesson that day,
never beat with sticks something big, puffy and gray.

LHC

Green Onions

Off to the garden we go,
with cold biscuits in tow.

Green onions with blades like straws,
between our biscuits we gnaw.

Sipping water through the blade like a straw,
we love our garden onions and all.

LHC

The Country Store

On a hot summer day, my sister and I,
were thirsting for our favorite orange Nehi.

We gathered our change and courage galore.
So, off through the woods to the old country store.

We climbed steep hills and down deep valleys with our ears attuned
to unwanted sounds that could mean our doom.

In the distance, cow bells rang, trees moaned, and the winds began to blow,
with just three more hills to go.

Out of breath and legs so spent,
we sat on a log old and bent.

The steepest hill was yet to come.
"Get up sister! Let's run!"

There in the distance we could see,
the old Cornwell Store beckoning to my sister and me.

The smells were delightful! Bologna and cheese!
Big giant cookies in jars to please!

In the corner by the door
is what we'd been waiting for.

We raised the lid of the cooler so cold
and plucked out our Nehi the color of gold!

We spent our change and headed for home,
back through the woods we would roam.

Feeling brave having gone through the woods to the old country store,
with Nehi in our bags and so much more.

Moaning trees, the cowbells ring, no longer an alarm,
we are content headed back to the farm.

LHC

The Hickory Nut Tree

Oh Hickory Nut Tree you stand so tall;
your branches outstretched to shade us all.
We played beneath you all day long,
cracking your nuts and playing ball.

How old are you Hickory Nut Tree?
Seems you have always been there for me.
Many a flood tried to wash you away,
but your strong trunk refused to obey.

There is none as lovely as you,
so strong, yet graceful too.
Oh Hickory Nut Tree who stands all alone
in Clay Ballard's field you belong.

How I wish you could talk oh tree,
to remind us of the good times beneath thee.
Keep standing dear old tree,
for I miss you, you see.

Guard over your field tree,
for it belonged to Grandpa Clay and means a lot to me.
Stand tall Hickory Nut Tree, and hold your branches strong,
for I am coming to see you before the summer's gone.

LHC

The Hog Lot

Wouldn't it just be, that the finest apple tree
is in the hog lot out of reach of me.

We kids sat on the fence like birds in a row,
staring at the forbidden apple tree in the hog lot below.

Big giant hogs wandering through the lot guarding the apple tree,
while we dared each other to go look and see.

"How about you go really quick,
as we swat the hogs with our sticks?"

"The apple tree doesn't seem so far away
in the hog lot today."

Each dared the other to no avail,
so we climbed off the fence and turned tail.

"Tomorrow we will go," we say.
"Maybe the hogs will be farther away."

"Sure," we all agree.
"Tomorrow…" We will see.

LHC

Canning Time

Wood fire burning with a roar.
Black tub filled with jars of green bean, corn, and more.

Cardboard in between the jars
to prevent the cracking scars.

Breaking beans, shucking corn,
and swatting flies was the norm.

Apples, peaches, jellies, and jams, stored in the cellar from the
biting cold.
Oh, the canning time in the days of old.

Jars on the shelf all in a row,
proudly display their contents all a glow.

When winter storms come rolling in,
to the jars on the shelf, we look within.

They keep our bellies full—to our delights,
all throughout the winters' nights.

LHC

Secondhand Dresses

Off to school in my secondhand dress,
starched and ironed to look its best.

The clothes' room such a delight!
"May I have this one, Mom?" "Yes, you might!"

We took them home that very night,
to wear to school with our sashes in flight.

So proud to wear my secondhand dress.
Clothes lovingly cared for by mom and so beautifully pressed.

LHC

Little White School House

In a curve on the knoll
sits the little white schoolhouse from days of old.

Well-oiled floors black as tar,
with big, tall windows to see afar.

Full of desks and benches galore,
blackboards, erasers, chalk, and more.

The pot belly stove in the center did sit,
turning red from the fire that's lit.

Coal piled out back up against the wall,
waiting to warm us all.

Out houses labeled 'Boys' and 'Girls',
nestled against the woods with the squirrels.

The county nurse and her little black bag in tow,
with scary needles that made us run and go.

Bible man so sweet and kind,
Bible verses he taught us to read and find.

Fun at recess, games begin, playing Dare Base and ball!
Alas, until the teacher calls.

May Day programs with redbud limbs,
girls in white dresses who walk under them.

Fetching water just down the road,
to fill our paper cups to overflow.

Alice and Jerry books, little and blue,
our first-grade reader books smelled so new.

I miss that little white schoolhouse so long ago.
Glad you are in my memory always to hold.

LHC

Mad Dogs

It's evening and almost dark,
an eerie feeling as we embark.

Strange dogs coming out of the field.
Mouths are foaming! Daddy says, "They must be killed!"

"Hurry quick! Shut the porch gate!
Get my gun, before it's too late!"

Safe on the porch from the raging dogs,
Daddy put an end to their maddening fog.

LHC

Haunted House

Big white house sitting under the hill,
scary sounds that stopped us still.

Creaky stairs, unfamiliar sounds,
footsteps, but no one to be found.

Shadows in windows loomed.
Are they real? Or are we doomed?

Stories of haints and headless men,
Ladies in white dresses, hover over the ditch in the bend.

Tales of tickling feet in the dark of night,
blankets pulled off in a fright.

Tiny little men standing by our beds,
Are they real? Oh, what a dread!

The big white house under the hill,
stories are told that scare us still.

LHC

The Frightful Pot Belly Stove

Oh! The potbelly stove!
Surely a fright to behold.

It's red to the top as far as we can see.
Oh my, oh my! What's to be?

Flames a cracking, heat so warm,
kids all around the teacher swarm.

"Look, teacher," someone said, starring at the stove so red.
"What must we do?" We're filled with dread!

Red to the ceiling the pipe so tall.
Oh my! Oh my! Is it going to fall?

No! Not at all.
It's just another day at school, that's all.

LHC

Mammy's Christmas Tree

I walk the path to Mammy's House to see her Christmas tree.
Oh, what a delight for me!

Glass beads all around from top to bottom,
I wonder where she got them…

Bells and tinsel hanging down,
listening for their tinkling sound.

In the front room it did sit
with big bulbs brightly lit.

The beautiful tree so big to me,
so glad I went to see, Mammy's Christmas tree.

LHC

Christmas at Mom-maw's

It's Christmas Eve and time to go,
to Mom-maw's house through the snow.

Beneath the hill we arrive,
to Mom-maw's house way up high.

Windows all aglow and front door open wide,
welcoming us to come inside.

Pot belly stove burning bright.
Christmas tree in the window, oh what a sight!

Sparkling glass ornaments, twinkling tinsel too.
Oh, what a wonder for us to view!

Baskets of apples and oranges so sweet,
all tucked in corners so very neat.

Sideboard with many drawers and doors
kept hidden things like sweets and more!

Oh what a treat to be at Mom-maw's house on Christmas Eve,
but Santa is coming, we must take our leave.

LHC

Santa Clause and the Old Smokehouse

It's Christmas Eve and quiet as a mouse.
The snow is deep with footprints to the old Smokehouse.

Whose could they be? I wonder with pause.
My daddy says, "They must be Santa Clause."

"Don't go to the smokehouse," my daddy warned.
"For it's not good to see Santa before Christmas morn."

Night came early and I could not sleep,
thinking of footprints in the snow so deep.

Morning is here with such a great joy,
for under the trees are dolls and toys!

Still I wonder about those footprints in the snow so deep,
Was Santa in the smokehouse? Dare I take a peep?

LHC

Santa Clause and the Old Smokehouse

It's Christmas Eve and quiet as a mouse.
The snow is deep with footprints to the old Smokehouse.

Whose could they be? I wonder with pause.
My daddy says, "They must be Santa Clause."

"Don't go to the smokehouse," my daddy warned.
"For it's not good to see Santa before Christmas morn."

Night came early and I could not sleep,
thinking of footprints in the snow so deep.

Morning is here with such a great joy,
for under the trees are dolls and toys!

Still I wonder about those footprints in the snow so deep,
Was Santa in the smokehouse? Dare I take a peep?

LHC